# Motor Racing at
# Thruxton
## in the 1980s

VELOCE

## Also from Veloce –

**Those Were The Days ... Series**
Alpine Trials & Rallies 1910-1973 (Pfundner)
American 'Independent' Automakers – AMC to Willys 1945 to 1960 (Mort)
American Station Wagons – The Golden Era 1950-1975 (Mort)
American Trucks of the 1950s (Mort)
American Trucks of the 1960s (Mort)
American Woodies 1928-1953 (Mort)
Anglo-American Cars from the 1930s to the 1970s (Mort)
Austerity Motoring (Bobbitt)
Austins, The last real (Peck)
Brighton National Speed Trials (Gardiner)
British and European Trucks of the 1970s (Peck)
British Drag Racing – The early years (Pettitt)
British Lorries of the 1950s (Bobbitt)
British Lorries of the 1960s (Bobbitt)
British Touring Car Racing (Collins)
British Police Cars (Walker)
British Woodies (Peck)
Café Racer Phenomenon, The (Walker)

Drag Bike Racing in Britain – From the mid '60s to the mid '80s (Lee)
Dune Buggy Phenomenon, The (Hale)
Dune Buggy Phenomenon Volume 2, The (Hale)
Endurance Racing at Silverstone in the 1970s & 1980s (Parker)
Hot Rod & Stock Car Racing in Britain in the 1980s (Neil)
Last Real Austins 1946-1959, The (Peck)
MG's Abingdon Factory (Moylan)
Motor Racing at Brands Hatch in the Seventies (Parker)
Motor Racing at Brands Hatch in the Eighties (Parker)
Motor Racing at Crystal Palace (Collins)
Motor Racing at Goodwood in the Sixties (Gardiner)
Motor Racing at Nassau in the 1950s & 1960s (O'Neil)
Motor Racing at Oulton Park in the 1960s (McFadyen)
Motor Racing at Oulton Park in the 1970s (McFadyen)
Motor Racing at Thruxton in the 1970s (Grant-Braham)
Motor Racing at Thruxton in the 1980s (Grant-Braham)
Superprix – The Story of Birmingham Motor Race (Page & Collins)
Three Wheelers (Bobbitt)

# www.veloce.co.uk

First published in March 2012 by Veloce Publishing Limited, Veloce House, Parkway Farm Business Park, Middle Farm Way, Poundbury, Dorchester, Dorset, DT1 3AR, England.
Fax 01305 250479/e-mail info@veloce.co.uk/web www.veloce.co.uk or www.velocebooks.com.

ISBN: 978-1-845843-69-4 UPC: 6-36847-04369-8

Readers with ideas for automotive books, or books on other transport or related hobby subjects, are invited to write to the editorial director of Veloce Publishing at the above address.
British Library Cataloguing in Publication Data – A catalogue record for this book is available from the British Library.
Typesetting, design and page make-up all by Veloce Publishing Ltd on Apple Mac. Printed in India by Replika Press.

# Contents

# Acknowledgements

In researching this book I referred constantly to back-copies of *Autosport*, *Motorsport News* (aka *Motoring News*) and *MotorSport,* as well as the invaluable *Autocourse*. *Thruxton – The first 30 years* by Paul Lawrence was essential reading, as were *Motor Racing Directory* and *The Pace Motor Racing Directory* by Mike Kettlewell. Additional books dipped into, in no particular order, were: *A-Z of Formula Racing* by David Hodges; *Crashed and Byrned* by Tommy Byrne and Mark Hughes; *Life and Spice*, the autobiography of Gordon Spice; *Gerry Marshall, his authorised biography* by Jeremy Walton and Gregor Marshall; *Ayrton Senna – The hard edge of genius* by Christopher Hilton; *Eddie Jordan – An independent man – The autobiography*; *The Toleman Story – Last romantics in Formula One* by Christopher Hilton; *Formula One – Driver by Driver* by Alan Henry; *Drive it! The Complete Book of Formula Two motor racing* by Tristan Wood; and *Whizzo – The motor sporting life of Barrie Williams* by Paul Lawrence.

Dennis Carter of the British Automobile Racing Club (BARC) and his predecessor, the late Sidney Offord, have always been totally supportive of my efforts. Their colleagues – Mark Cole, Enid Smith, Dave Price, Trevor Swettenham, Bill Coombs, and the late Ian Taylor – all demonstrated unstinting patience.

## Dedication

This book is dedicated to Barbara, Danielle and Anika who deserve praise for accepting that their absentee husband/father was often ... at Thruxton!

# Introduction

Thruxton in the 1980s was a place of great excitement, and a major force in the evolution of motorsport. The circuit basked in the glory of the early F2 races, when grand prix drivers of the calibre of Rindt, Hill, Courage, Stewart, and Peterson, would relish testing the up-and-coming new racing talent away from the pressures of grand prix weekends.

All this was in Hampshire in the south of England where, since the demise of the BARC's Goodwood circuit, there had been little opportunity for locals to immerse themselves in top level motorsport.

For those who proudly declared themselves 'petrol

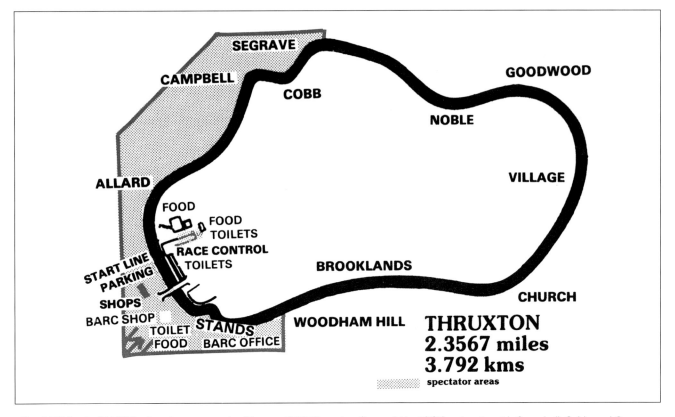

The 2.356 mile (3.792km) perimeter track of former RAF Thruxton formed the 1980s circuit, with Campbell, Cobb, and Segrave corners being known as 'The Complex.'

In the early '80s Easter Monday at Thruxton was synonymous with F2. The annual atmosphere of excitement was epitomised by the busy 1982 grid.

heads,' Thruxton quickly became a rural idyll. In his book *Ayrton Senna – the hard head of genius*, the late Christopher Hilton summed up the atmosphere perfectly by contrasting the Thruxton circuit with a street race in the Chinese city of Macau:

"Thruxton, settled in the gentility of English pastureland, has no slums, no casinos, and you have to buy rice in packets from the corner shop; but for a motor race it's as good a place as any, and better than most. Those who come to Thruxton – to drive, watch, or parade as officials – care."

The wide open expanses of Thruxton's tarmac are neither a genteel drive in the countryside nor a walk in a park, as the many who have driven the circuit in anger will readily testify. The circuit is certainly distinctive. It's fast – very fast – and over the years its only UK rivals

By 1986 Interserie sportscars were the Easter stars. 1985 Le Mans winner 'John Winter' (Louis Klages) flew in his Porsche 956C.

for speed were the original Snetterton Norwich straight layout, and Silverstone with its Hangar straight. During the 1980s, though, Thruxton was the fastest race on the European F2 Championship calendar, even against competition from the likes of Hockenheim.

Setting up a competition car for Thruxton is always a compromise between the two slow sections and the long flat-out sweeps in the direction of Thruxton village. There are no real straights, and, as a result, tyre wear is invariably a problem. The constant high-speed cornering – in 2.356 miles (3.792km) there are only two diminutive straights either side of Cobb corner at 'The Complex,' and even these are properly attacked in arcs – means that there is never time for any real cooling to take place, whatever the type of racing.

During the early '80s Thruxton was criticised for its lack of proper pits and a paddock, as well as for its bumpiness – which was thought to have been a

7

An iconic Thruxton 'Grand Prix nursery' graduate was Ayrton Senna, here hurling his damaged F3 Ralt through Club in 1983.

contributory factor in Mike Thackwell's horrific 1981 F2 accident. The pits were certainly primitive by modern standards. By 1984, *Autosport's* iconic F2 reporter, Ian Phillips, was describing Allard corner as "corrugated," and Segrave as a "yump." That same year one of the drivers who knew most about the consequences of getting off-line at Thruxton took F2 pole. Mike Thackwell yet again demonstrated his unique approach by simply

driving around the bumps! In 1984, the new pits complex opened, and the notorious bump at Church was ironed out before the start of the 1985 season. For 1987, the entire circuit was resurfaced, and work on improved spectator banking was begun.

The start of the 1980 season revealed that the central Club Corner Armco had been replaced by high kerbs and catch fencing. There would be no more

*Andy Rouse and Gordon Spice's BTCC Capris didn't seem affected by any bumpiness at Allard corner in 1980.*

shooting the whites of the drivers' eyes from that precarious position.

More so than most activities, motorsport is vulnerable to the economic realities of the outside world. At the beginning of the decade Thruxton, and many of the Championships it hosted, relied on attracting commercial backing from a UK economy that was characterised by rising unemployment and reduced manufacturing capacity. Prime Minister Margaret Thatcher and Chancellor Geoffrey Howe attempted to address the situation by increasing taxes and reducing government spending. Money was tight, and there was even civil unrest. Not the ideal atmosphere in which to attract sponsorship.

Teams were increasingly looking closely at their costs, and before the circuit's 1982 F2 race there was some carping about the unofficial four-hour Thursday practice session held prior to Easter. Attendance for this could require as many as six nights in hotels, making Thruxton the most expensive F2 race on the calendar! By 1984, the unofficial Thursday practice had been scrapped, but, ironically, by the time European F3000 arrived for 1985 there was criticism of the lack of testing time!

In the early 1980s, F2 was still feeding teams and drivers directly into F1, as evidenced by the Toleman, Spirit and Minardi teams, to name but three. Gradually, though, F2 was coming under threat as F3 became an alternative proving ground for future F1 drivers. F3 visited Thruxton on as many as five separate occasions during a season to showcase drivers of the calibre of Martin Brundle and Ayrton Senna, for whom F1 was already beckoning.

So, what happened at Thruxton during the 1980s? The Thruxton Easter F2 event initially prospered, but was replaced by European F3000 in 1985. When this proved too expensive in 1986, Interserie sports cars arrived, but financial success eluded the BARC. From then on F3 came into its own, and, following a dip, the British Touring Car Championship started to stage a revival.

Where drivers were concerned, the likes of Martin Brundle, Damon Hill, and the introverted Ayrton Senna climbed the ladder out of the Thruxton nursery to F1 stardom. Inexplicably, some obvious talent didn't make it, prominent examples being Tommy Byrne and Mike Thackwell. Many others were learning the ropes and would become household names in the following decade – the likes of Eddie Irvine, David Coulthard, Mika Hakkinen and Alan McNish.

Bruce Grant-Braham, PhD, Director,
Motorsport Research Group,
Bournemouth University

*Just four months into the new decade Brian Henton lowered the lap record in his immaculate F2 BP Toleman-Hart TG280.*

# Outright record holders

As one of the fastest tracks in the country Thruxton's outright circuit record always carries a special cachet. Requiring a perfectly set-up car, strong neck muscles, and a mix of both experience and bravery, an outright record holder inevitably walks tall in the sport.

During the 1980s, the track provided fewer opportunities to produce records than had been originally anticipated, due to the limited number of permitted events. Inevitably, the quality grand prix-level drivers in F2 would dominate before its decline, and then the power of the Ford Cosworth DFV would kick in with the creation of F3000.

The four drivers who raised the lap speed by 8.77mph (14.113kph) during the decade are all big names in motorsport, with Thruxton being an essential addition to their CVs.

### Brian Henton, 7th April 1980
*Toleman-Hart TG280 – 122.85mph/197.7kph – 1m09.04s*

A successful businessman from Castle Donington near Derby, Brian had already had a few F1 outings with March and Lotus in the 1970s – having won the 1977 race – by the time he came to Thruxton in 1980. Driving the pristine Pirelli radial-shod BP Toleman-Hart TG280 for the opening F2 race of the season, he was unable to avoid a spinning Manfred Winkelhock (March-BMW 802) at Church in unofficial practice. This was after having already had a rear wheel come loose. He started from third place on the grid and, early on, watched his pole-sitting team-mate, Derek Warwick, fight with Andrea de Cesaris (Project 4 March-BMW 802) only for the latter's Goodyear tyres to expire. Many others experienced the same problem, and Toleman had been concerned when, in the warm-up, Warwick's intended race tyres had blistered after only five laps. In the end Henton enjoyed superior grip to just about everyone else and, after 55 laps, led home a popular Toleman one-two.

*Marc Surer regained the record in 1981 using Japanese Dunlop tyres on his F2 March BMW. He had the smoothest of styles through Club.*

### Marc Surer, 20th April 1981
*March 812 – 124.73mph/200.7kph – 1m08.00s*

Swiss driver Marc Surer had previously taken Thruxton's outright record (122.73 mph/197.5kph – 1m09.11s) during his European F2 Championship year of 1979. It would take him two years to wrestle the accolade back from Brian Henton. In the intervening period Marc had become an F1 driver with both Ensign and ATS, but his nemesis was to be Kyalami where he suffered a bad accident in practice in 1980 (breaking his ankle). Unusually, he was the only user of Japanese Dunlop tyres in Thruxton's 1981 Easter F2 race. These enabled him to place Markus Hotz's understeering Horag March BMW/Heidegger 812 into third place on the grid, behind Thierry Boutsen (March 812) and Geoff Lees (Ralt-Honda RH6-81). Onlookers observed that he was notably smoother than the others through the chicane. In the race, Surer chased Boutsen and overtook Kenny Acheson (Toleman) before the former's engine blew. This put Marc into the lead until his Dunlops started to go off around lap 33, whereupon Robert Guerrero's Maurer-BMW inherited first spot. Surer's Heidegger engine eventually gave out shortly before the end of the 55 laps, and he disconsolately parked by the track with only the outright record as reward for his determination.

*Despite a Michelin tyre exploding, Venezuelan motorcycle Champion Johnny Cecotto took the record whilst fighting back from the resulting pit stop.*

### Johnny Cecotto, 12th April 1982
*March 882 – 125.90mph/202.6kph – 1m07.37s*

The former motorcycle World Champion – in both 350cc and 750cc – swapped two wheels for four when he moved to F2 in 1981 with Minardi. For 1982 the Venezuelan teamed up with eventual European F2 Champion Corrado Fabi and Christian Danner in works Onyx-run March cars. He finished in runner-up spot at the end of the year, having won the Easter P&O Ferries race at Thruxton on the way. Durable tyres were in short supply on that cold, sunny day. Hard Michelin tyres seemed to be the way to go for Johnny until his left front exploded around Goodwood, dropping him from fourth to fourteenth and forcing a pit stop. A determined recovery drive through the field saw him capitalise on others' tyre problems – as well as Fabi's stone-damaged distributor. He resisted a late challenge from Stefan Johansson's Spirit and gained the outright lap record, which remained in place for seven years.

## Roland Ratzenberger, 27th March 1989
*Reynard 88D – 131.62mph/211.8kph – 1m04.44s*

The likeable Austrian Roland Ratzenberger lowered the track record during the second 1989 round of the fledgling domestic British F3000 Championship. He was driving a Spirit Motorsport Reynard 88D powered by a Nicholson 450bhp Ford DFV F1 engine. Roland headed row two in a race that boasted a mere ten entries. He chased and overtook early race leader Andrew Gilbert-Scott, only for his DFV to prove temperamental allowing eventual race winner Gary Brabham past. Roland may have finished a battling second in the 40-lap race, but he popped the circuit record into his pocket and it saw out the decade.

In 1989 Roland Ratzenberger (16) pressed race winner Gary Brabham's F3000 Reynard 88D, and for the first time raised the lap record above 130mph (209.2kmh).

# Easter Monday
# – it must be Thruxton

During the 1970s, the accepted place for British motorsport enthusiasts on Easter Bank Holiday Monday had unquestionably become Thruxton, and its Formula Two race. This national tradition would endure well into the 1980s.

### F2 – 1980

For Thruxton's 12th annual F2 race, the patriots were happy, for chief amongst the 2-litre F2 contenders was a new British car with two British drivers, a flagship British sponsor, and a British team threatening a future in F1. What's more, its tyre supplier, Pirelli, was known to have similar aspirations.

The team was Toleman, and the BP-backed car the TG280. Team principal Alex Hawkridge decided, in mid-1979, to become a constructor, and the design experience of Rory Byrne and John Gentry came up with a clever, Hart-powered blueprint to guide BS Fabrications. Having overcome understeer, the sleek cars dominated the 1980 season, thanks not only to their amazingly reliable Hart engines, but also to the way the restriction on side skirts was handled. The rules stated that they could be no lower than the driver's seat. Byrne's solution was to drop the seat through the base of the monocoque; it worked a treat at Thruxton.

The anticipated all-British driver line-up was expected to be Derek Warwick and Stephen South. Whilst Toleman was testing the TG280 at Vallelunga, however, under the eyes of the Pirelli hierarchy, South was driving an F1 McLaren at Paul Ricard. The Toleman

Alresford driver Derek Warwick awaits the off in his pristine BP-backed TG280 in 1980. The low level seat was the winning Rory Byrne design feature.

team was not amused, and he was replaced by Thruxton-favourite and previous F2 winner Brian Henton.

Once the team had got its act together – Hawkridge had been critical of its cohesion during practice – Brian led home an apparently effortless record-breaking one-two in the race (see Chapter 1). At season's end Brian and Derek topped the European F2 Championship, and F1 beckoned for the Toleman Group; building upon lessons learned from the TG280 and the Hart engine. When F2 returned to Thruxton in 1981 it was in the same week that Derek Warwick was testing the prototype F1 Toleman-Hart turbo at Silverstone.

The lead trio. Derek Warwick bursts out of Club, leading Andrea de Cesaris' March and Brian Henton early in the 1980 F2 race.

Race winner Henton watches as his team-mate, Derek Warwick, sprays the champagne for second place. Alex Hawkridge, the bearded Toleman boss, looks on proudly.

## F2 – 1981

Unfortunately, legal issues arose at Thruxton for the eventual winners. The Gustav Brunner-designed Mampe Maurer MM81s of Robert Guerrero and Eje Elgh took a one-two, only to be protested by all the leading teams. The controversy surrounded the centre body section of the F1 standard car, and whether or not it acted as a sliding skirt. The situation was so complicated that it was referred to FISA's Technical Committee, but no sanctions were ever applied. Second placed Eje Elgh's black Maurer was additionally disqualified as his rear wing end plates were deemed too high at race end – due to accident damage according to team manager Paul Owens. Much later, Elgh was re-instated following an appeal, although the team was fined.

A superb entry of 28 cars arrived for the third round of the FIA European F2 Championship in which Marc Surer took the lap record (See Chapter 1). The story of the meeting was one of tyres, with Bridgestone, Dunlop, Pirelli, and M&H all fighting each other. Thierry Boutsen's March BMW 812 took pole for Bridgestone. BMW engines dominated, despite Honda's refined V6 producing

*The start of F2's engine war and the road to F1 for Honda. The Japanese F2 engine took on the BMWs and soon dominated.*

Both controversial Mampe Maurer MM81s were protested in 1981. Eje Elgh's rear wing end plates caused his disqualification from second place – he was later reinstated.

Geoff Lees was the sole Ralt-Honda RH6-81 driver at Thruxton following Mike Thackwell's severe accident in practice. Geoff would be 1981 European Champion.

Young German sensation Stefan Bellof initially led the 1982 Championship, having won at Silverstone and Hockenheim. At Thruxton, though, engine failure halted his successful run.

.Future Ferrari F1 driver Michele Alboreto in the cockpit of his Faenza-built 1981 Minardi FLY281. The team, too, was rehearsing for F1.

325-330 bhp – allegedly 10 per cent more than the BMW and Hart opposition. Mike Thackwell's nasty Goodwood corner accident in unofficial practice – which left him unconscious for three days – left second on the grid Geoff Lees (stepping back from F1 and lucrative sports car offers) as the sole Ralt-Honda RH6-81 driver in Hampshire. He completed only 40 of the 55 laps due to electrical and tyre problems, but he went on to be European F2 Champion, underlining the domination of Honda.

*Damaged electrics denied birthday boy Corrado Fabi an easy win in his works Roloil March 822 in 1982.*

### F2 – 1982

Japanese domination was expected this year, but the Honda engine developed by Geoff Lees was not as good as expected. This power plant appeared in the Ralt Honda Team (RH6/82H) of Lees and Kenny Acheson, as well as the fledgling Spirit Honda Team of Stefan Johansson and Thierry Boutsen.

BMW had almost pulled out of F2, having conducted limited development of its M12 4-cylinder engine, upon which the March works team of Corrado Fabi, Johnny Cecotto and Christian Danner depended. Despite this, the Ralf Bellamy-designed March 822 – narrower than its predecessor, lighter, running improved aerodynamics and rear suspension – won at

Pole-sitter Stefan Johansson, Corrado Fabi, and Johnny Cecotto roar off the grid at the head of 28 F2 cars in 1982.

At the end of the first lap the leaders dodge inside Thierry Tassin's mangled Toleman-Hart DS1, after his spectacular Armco-rattling startline accident.

Thruxton, and, in the hands of Cecotto, took the circuit record, and eventually gave Corrado Fabi the European Championship.

On his 21st birthday, Corrado (Roloil March) looked set to win at Thruxton by a huge margin until electrical failure intervened. For Cecotto, this was the first of three wins, and of March's eight F2 wins of 1982.

Sheer BARC marshal manpower moves Tassin's battered Toleman to the side of the track. Safety cars had not been invented in 1982!

21

### Spirit Racing

Spirit Racing was formed in 1981 by former BARC Competition Secretary and March manager John Wickham, along with Gordon Coppuck, who had also been at March and previously McLaren. Its first car was the F2 201, which, in 1982, proved to be very competitive. Boasting Marlboro sponsorship, Honda engines, and Bridgestone tyres, the team's budget was sufficient to attract drivers of the calibre of Stefan Johansson and Thierry Boutsen.

Gordon Coppuck and John Wickham – formerly with the BARC at Thruxton – debut their Spirit 201 in F2 testing in February 1982. F1 was beckoning.

The 201 had a conventional aluminium honeycombe monocoque, which was initially prone to understeer. It was constructed around Honda's RA series 2-litre V6, but the overall package was sometimes frustratingly unreliable in its first season. Thierry Boutsen won three races, and was third in the Championship, with Stefan Johansson often blisteringly quick, taking pole on five of the first eight opportunities.

The fourth 201 chassis was adapted to F1 specification for a debut in the 1983 Race of Champions at Brands Hatch, with a Honda RA163-E turbo engine. The significance of Spirit Racing was that it led to the eventual return of Honda to F1.

Happy-go-lucky Swede Stefan Johansson had already driven for Shadow in F1 and won the Vandervell British F3 Championship before racing for Spirit in F2.

Whilst challenging for the lead, Stefan Johansson's Spirit spun into the Segrave bank on the penultimate 1982 lap as a wheel nut flew away.

In 1983 Siena-driver Alessandro Nannini heads a slipstreaming bunch of F2 cars in his Minardi 283. He was actually getting airborne over the Church bump.

### F2 – 1983

Beppe Gabbiani (March-BMW/Rosche 832) won four of the first five European F2 Championship races for Onyx, including round two at Thruxton, during which he was recovering from flu.

Honda was turning the thumbscrews, requiring a return for its F2 investment, and, in response, Mike Thackwell promptly took the Thruxton pole for Ralt-Honda in his Casio-sponsored RH6/83H. The engine was happily pulling 11,500rpm around the back of the circuit – 700rpm more than normal. He earned great praise on his return to the track which had nearly ended his career in 1981. Such was the competitiveness of the field that the first twelve cars qualified within a second of each other.

Thackwell romped off into the distance in the race, but, as usual, tyres played their part, and Gabbiani (Michelin), who had started eighth, played the rubber game perfectly to inherit the lead when Thackwell's left rear wore out after 37 laps. Ralt took the third place on the podium, thanks to Jonathan Palmer who later became the 1983 Champion with five wins in the last five races. Palmer's Thruxton experience, during which he had a frustrating practice, was the first of 11 successive finishes, such was Ralt-Honda's reliability.

Remembering the Maurer's 1981 problems, it was interesting that FISA officials chose Thruxton to experiment with a laser system, situated between Church and Club, to measure the ground clearance of the F2 cars, but never publicly declared the results.

Former Osella Squadra Corse F1 driver and another Italian, the decidedly unwell Beppe Gabbiani, won the 1983 race in his works March-BMW.

*Jonathan Palmer came third in 1983 in his F2 Ralt RH6/83 which boasted 340bhp of Honda power. He won the European F2 Championship, too.*

*West Sussex racer Jonathan Palmer had learned the correct Thruxton lines from his Modsports, Formula Ford, and Championship-winning F3 days (pictured here).*

### Jonathan Palmer

Jonathan was an engineering student, the son of a well known motor racing doctor, who later followed his father into medicine. Having attended the Brands Hatch Racing School, Jonathan raced a Sprite and then a 3-litre Marcos GT in which he took 27 wins – including three at Thruxton between 1976 and 1977 – before running very successfully in Formula Ford. He qualified as a doctor at Guy's Hospital Medical School in 1979, and then, in 1981, took a sabbatical from medicine to race in F3 with West Surrey Racing, winning the British Championship. He landed the Ralt-Honda F2 drive and tested for Williams before making his F1 debut for Williams at the European Grand Prix at Brands Hatch.

By the time he raced in F2, Jonathan Palmer was already renowned for his meticulous approach of setting his quickest time early in qualifying, before perfecting his car set-up by preparing settings for any situations that might occur in the race. Following an F1 career of 84 races (with Ram, Zakspeed and Tyrrell) and a spell as a BBC TV commentator, Jonathan eventually became one of the most powerful individuals in British motorsport – the Chief Executive of MotorSport Vision, the owner/operator of Brands Hatch, Oulton Park, Snetterton and Cadwell Park, as well as Bedford Autodrome.

Using his huge Motor Racing Developments knowledge Ralt genius Kiwi Ron Tauranac (left) shares a joke with Jonathan Palmer in Thruxton's very basic pits.

*1984 Champion Mike Thackwell starts from Thruxton's pole, with Christian Danner just behind, on a day when the correct tyre choice was extra important.*

### F2 – 1984

This was Mike Thackwell's year. In what turned out to be the final season of F2 he became both European Champion for Ralt-Honda as well as winning Thruxton in his Casio-sponsored RH6/84. Ralt's budget had allowed for a stiffer chassis than previously, and for the aerodynamics to be honed in the Williams Grand Prix wind tunnel. The engine installation was improved, too.

*Thruxton's last F2 podium with (left-to-right) Christian Danner, Mike Thackwell, and Philippe Streiff, acknowledging the plaudits. Financial storm clouds were brewing.*

Ralt was supremely successful making great use of the Michelin tyres as it won seven of the 11 races, took nine fastest laps, and six pole positions. Such was his dominance that many onlookers felt that Mike Thackwell was a future World Champion in the making.

The Ralts made use of the hardest tyre compounds possible at Thruxton, but Thackwell's team-mate Roberto Moreno's car succumbed to a wheel bearing failure. Away from the front of the grid F2 was struggling, with only 17 cars appearing at Thruxton for the BARC's 16th and final F2 Easter Monday race. There were no more Maurers, Spirits, or Martinis. Christian Danner was the leading challenger (March-BMW/Mader 842) and he'd looked certain to take pole at Thruxton until pipped by Thackwell. Using a mix of Michelin tyre compounds, Danner finished second. Phillipe Streiff qualified third in his distinctive AGS-BMW/Mader JH19C, and actually led the first lap. He survived a final lap spin to take the last place on the podium.

At the end of a brilliantly sunny afternoon, the combination of Easter Monday, Formula Two, and Thruxton finally parted company.

Mike Thackwell's progress stalled after this serious 1981 Thruxton practice accident. On his return, it didn't seem to affect his approach to the circuit.

### Mike Thackwell

New Zealander Mike Thackwell was born into a racing family, his father, Ray, having raced in speedway and then F2 as a privateer in the 1950s. Mike graduated through the junior levels of motorsport – karts and FF1600 – before making his mark in the 1979 British F3 Championship with five victories – including Thruxton's Championship Finals event. In 1980, he tested an Ensign whilst also racing for the works ICI March F2 team. He failed to qualify for Arrows (standing in for the injured Jochen Mass) in the Dutch GP, but in Canada, at the age of 19, he briefly drove a Tyrrell to become the youngest driver ever to start a World Championship Grand Prix. By 1984, he had created such a rapport within the Ralt-Honda F2 team that the combination became virtually unbeatable.

Back behind an F3000 wheel in 1985 Mike Thackwell came second to Emanuelle Pirro. But for his nose cone he could so easily have won.

### F3000 – 1985

Mike Thackwell's impeccable Thruxton record continued into 1985 when, using a Ralt RB20, he contested the headline Easter European F3000 race. The car used the F2 honeycomb chassis and front suspension, but was powered by a Judd DFV – this was the FIA F2-replacement formula that made use of a host of otherwise redundant F1 Ford Cosworth DFV engines. Thackwell put the red and white Bridgestone-backed car on pole. The other red and white cars at the front were the Marlboro Onyx March 85Gs of Michel Ferte and Emanuele Pirro. All were updated F2 designs.

As the race start approached the weather alternated between rain and sunshine, and so tyre choice involved an extra gamble. In the end, Pirro and Thackwell got it right with slicks, but the latter ruined his chances when he needed a pit stop to change a damaged nosecone. In charging back to threaten for the lead his helmet visor broke, meaning he had to drive much of the lap one-handed, eventually finishing second to Pirro.

Christian Danner (Bob Sparshott Automotive March) took the title at year end, but this would be the last visit of the European F3000 circus to Thruxton, as the financial loss made by the BARC could not be afforded again in 1986. The Club looked at sports cars for the following Easter.

### Interserie sports cars – 1986

For most casual onlookers the thrill of Interserie sports cars in 1986 surrounded the pace of the two race-winning Porsches and whether or not they would beat Johnny Cecotto's circuit record. Richard Lloyd Racing brought its 956C, which had come second at Le Mans in 1985, for James Weaver. Jonathan Palmer and Steve Soper offered advice from the pits. Suffering tyre problems in the first of the two races Weaver buckled down in the second and reeled in a series of blistering laps that got him to within 0.11s of the lap record. To give an idea of the velocities involved, the 900bhp 3-litre Porsche 962 of race one winner Jo Gartner was recorded as pulling 186mph (300kph) up Woodham Hill. Hidden under their respective sports car bodies in the meagre 15-car entry were former F2 chassis familiar to Thruxton in the form of a Maurer MM82 – once raced by Stefan Bellof – a Ralt RT2, a Spirit 201, and a March-BMW 832.

*The damp pole position lap of Austrian Jo Gartner. Despite the conditions his mighty Kremer Porsche 962C was clocked at 186mph (300kph) up Woodham Hill!*

# Formula Three

During the 1980s, F3 – which was for single-seater cars with 2-litre engines boasting a 24mm restrictor plate – became increasingly important as a source of future grand prix drivers. This was thanks in part to the 1981 arrival of series sponsor Marlboro, which, through its connections, was able to dangle F1 test drives in front of the up-and-coming. It was Thruxton's good luck that it frequently hosted the final British Championship race of the season when such rewards were decided.

Nigel Mansell impressed in his F3 March in 1980. Before the year was out he would debut for Lotus F1 at the Austrian Grand Prix.

## 1980

For the final year of the Vandervell British F3 Championship, March was under pressure, as both Argo and Ralt chassis came good, but sometimes as few as 14 cars sometimes raced as the recession bit hard. Thruxton's year was characterised by some very hairy high-speed spins around the back of the circuit, by several of the leading contenders.

The Argo JM6 was particularly suited to Thruxton. Roberto Guerrero scored the constructor's first ever F3 win in March in his Anglia Cars/Caribou Jeans version, and the Colombian then led an Argo one-two in May ahead of Thierry Tassin. Other F3 victors included the popular Ulsterman Kenny Acheson (RMC 793) in April, and Stefan Johansson in October. The impressive Swede had started the year in his Project 4 March 803, but was driving a Ralt RT3 by season's end. Of those who persevered with the March, both Nigel Mansell and Eddie Jordan usually finished well in Hampshire.

Kenny Acheson's April win came about when Brett Riley, thinking the race to be over, had mistakenly pulled in to the pits early (eventually finishing fourth in the pit lane!), and Johansson had squandered his pole when his engine stuttered at the start.

At the exciting 20th and final race of the Championship, Guerrero, Acheson, and Johansson all came to Thruxton with three wins apiece. Johansson took the Vandervell title by two points as his Ralt's aerodynamics, which included the team's self-designed, single-post rear wing, worked to perfection.

Rob Wilson (Ralt RT3) won the popular non-Championship BBC TV race in November.

(Opposite, top) County Tyrone racer Kenny Acheson (left) was popular with the Thruxton crowd, as was fellow Irishman – and now TV pundit – Eddie Jordan.

(Opposite, bottom) The Argo JM6 was the car to beat in 1980, and here Colombian Roberto Guerrero proves the point, heading Kenny Acheson and the rest.

### 1981

Over the winter Johansson's victorious 1980 Ralt RT3 chassis was purchased for Jonathan Palmer, and run by Dick Bennett's West Surrey Racing (WSR). During a dominant season, Palmer entered 20 races and attended 35 test sessions, enabling him to hone his legendary car sorting ability.

Having won Silverstone's opening F3 round, Palmer tested at Goodwood, because that circuit's characteristics were so similar to those of Thruxton. Despite being affected by wind shear through Goodwood and Church corners, he achieved a crushing round two win.

Belgian Thierry Tassin took the April and October F3 victories as well as the lap record (1m13.93s; 114.72mph/184.62kph). In the first of these, David Leslie had been on pole, but Tassin overtook the Scot when he missed a gear. Earlier, Palmer had recorded his only

*Jonathan Palmer's 1981 Ralt RT3 WSR chassis was actually the 1980 Championship-winning car of Stefan Johansson.*

South African, Mike White, won an important victory for March in early May. Here, he has only Thierry Tassin ahead of him at Campbell.

F3 was increasingly becoming a fruitful hunting ground for F1 talent scouts, including Frank Williams who visited Thruxton in October 1981.

retirement of the season, having become caught up in a first lap melee – getting airborne at the Complex. In the wet and cold October round Palmer could only finish sixth, his car suffering from tyre and gearbox ailments. The promising Dave Scott (Ralt RT3/81) had been on pole, and eventually finished third. He stood atop the podium after the non-Championship Canon Copiers BBC TV race in November, and took a new F3 lap record (1m13.56s; 115.30mph/185.55kph).

South African Mike White took a popular win in May in his works March 813. This was to prove to be the last works March F3 win. His only problem had been a bird strike coming up Woodham Hill towards the end of the race, but luckily he'd built up a sufficient cushion on Thierry Tassin when feathers blocked up his engine's air intake, smothering its performance.

### 1982

In what was to be his Championship year, Tommy Byrne racked up two Thruxton wins. In March, Dave Scott jumped the start and, on the slippery track, Byrne's Shell-backed Ralt RT3C/81 – with Hesketh-built Toyota power – was the class of the field. Another victory followed in April. In October, Martin Brundle took his BP-sponsored Dave Price Ralt VW to a well-earned win. An understeering Byrne, who had missed three races thanks to F1 commitments with Theodore, and his closest challenger, Argentinean 'Quique' Mansilla, had been the focus of attention. On wet tyres Byrne held off Mansilla at the chicane to take the overall Championship victory. Curiously, during the year Mansilla had made use of the same Ralt WSR chassis that had previously taken both Johansson and Palmer to their titles. Mansilla had also had to cope with the wider personal implications of the Falklands conflict.

Rally ace Henri Toivonen made his F3 debut in the October race, and appeared again for the non-Championship November BBCTV meeting, which boasted the largest F3 field of the year: 26 cars. Impressively, he finished fourth, having needed his rally skills to survive a grassy moment at Club. He was off to the RAC Rally the following weekend. Ayrton Senna da Silva achieved a debut F3 win, in a portent of what was to come in 1983.

*Tommy Byrne blasts away from pole in the first race of 1982. He had to win to fund his next race; he did.*

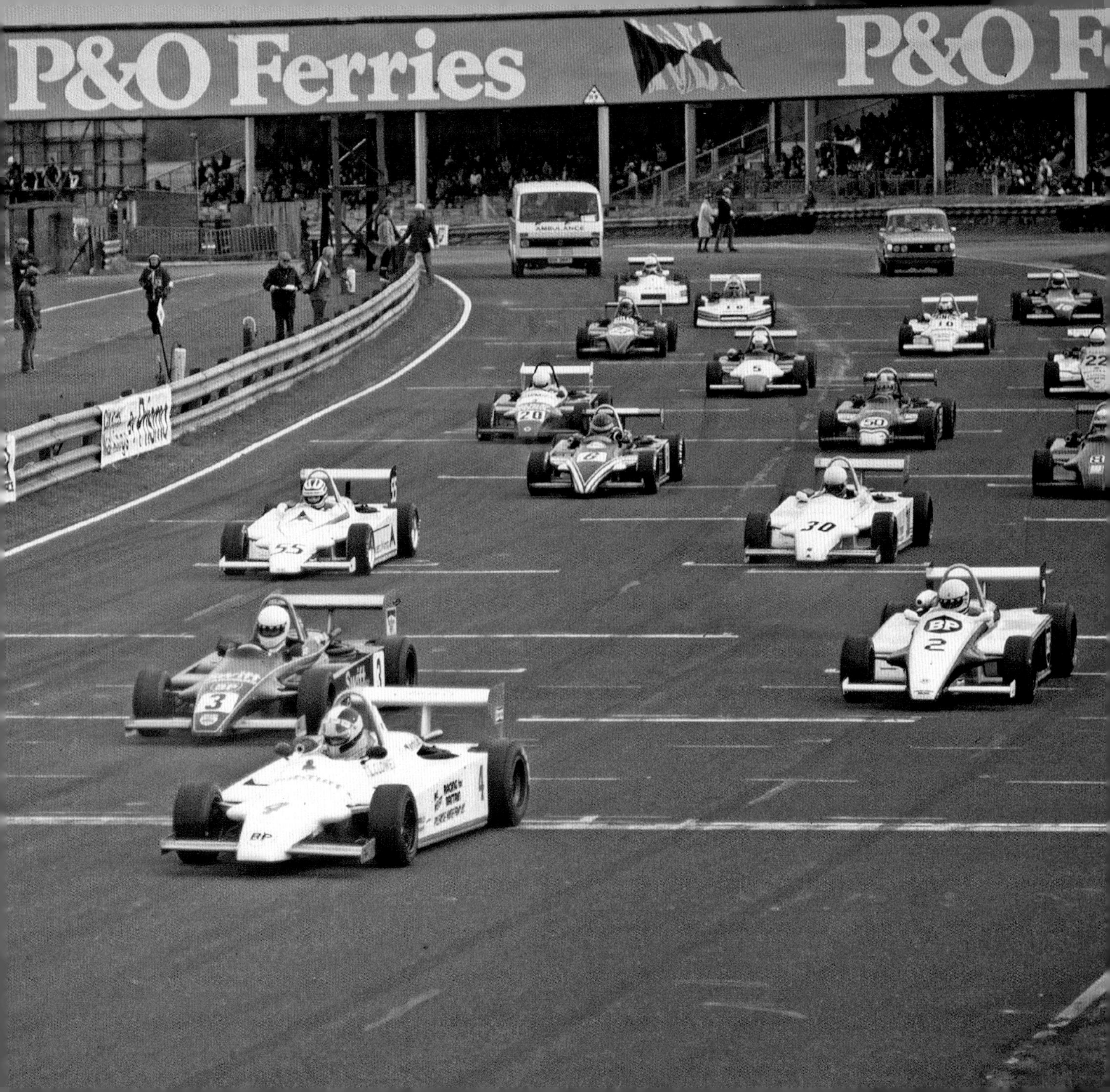
P&O Ferries
P&O F
AMBULANCE

Martin Brundle – future F1 driver and TV pundit – sits expectantly on pole in his BP-sponsored Dave Price Ralt-VW.

Both Dave Scott (3) and Richard Trott were stalwarts of the UK's club racing system. As a result they knew all of Thruxton's idiosyncrasies.

Tommy Byrne flies through Club in November 1982 showing his characteristic steely car control and pace.

### Tommy Byrne and Ayrton Senna

Already an established Champion in FF1600 and FF2000, Tommy Byrne, the likeable Irishman from Dundalk, had replaced his rival – the temporarily 'retired' Ayrton Senna – and won the 1981 Formula Ford Festival at Brands Hatch in the Brazilian's car. Tommy's prize was a Murray Taylor-inspired Marlboro-backed

Thruxton F3 race at season's end. On that November day an impressive Tommy broke the lap record in qualifying and ran a close second to Dave Scott in the race. But for a damaged undertray he might have won the non-Championship event.

Some felt that there was more to the absence of Senna than met the eye, and subsequently there was

Enrique Mansilla, Martin Brundle and Tommy Byrne celebrate in November 1982.

surprise when the Brazilian moved into FF2000 with Dennis Rushen in 1982, instead of F3 where Tommy would continue to impress. Allegations persisted that Tommy was the sole individual that Ayrton perceived could rival his reputation, hence his reluctance at this stage in his career to go head-to-head.

Tommy's financially precarious 1982 F3 season started with a win at Silverstone, which, luckily, yielded the funds for the second race at Thruxton. Again, he had to win to generate cash for Murray Taylor's team; he promptly dominated. This was to be the scenario throughout what would be his hand-to-mouth British

Tommy's (1) racing education included battling Roberto Moreno and Jonathan Palmer in Formula Ford at Thruxton in 1980.

... and doing the same (red car) against Dave Coyne (81) in FF2000 in 1981.

In 1982, rally driver Henri Toivonen (right) proved that he could easily have been a top racing driver. Here, he swaps experiences with Stefan Johansson.

F3 Championship-winning year, which included another Thruxton win. His prize this time would be a McLaren F1 test, but he didn't hold out any hopes as Jonathan Palmer had received the same prize a year earlier and nothing had come from that. Tommy had already been invited to meet McLaren's Ron Dennis after his first Hampshire success, but would actually make his F1 debut during 1982 with Theodore at the German GP. Inexplicably, considering his obvious talent behind the wheel, his grand prix career fizzled out that very same year, after just two grand prix starts.

### 1983

The 1983 F3 season was all about the dominance of Ayrton Senna (WSR) and Martin Brundle (Eddie Jordan Racing), with the Brazilian failing to get everything his own way as had originally been anticipated. This was despite Eddie Jordan's team and Brundle doing well to recover from the fatal accident that befell their transporter in Austria in mid-season. The only Thruxton interloper in the Senna/Brundle rivalry was American teenager Davy Jones who won the now traditional but last non-Championship televised race in November – his first F3 win.

### Ayrton Senna and Martin Brundle

Back in 1981, Brazilian kart racer Ayrton Senna da Silva – nicknamed 'Harry' by his team – had first appeared at Thruxton in the opening round of the Townsend Thoresen FF1600 Championship with a works Van Diemen RF81. Watched by his beautiful wife Liliane, he finished third behind Rick Morris and Enrique Mansilla. In a portent of what was to come, in August he clinched the Townsend Thoresen title at Thruxton, following his sixth win of the season, accompanied by his signature pole position and fastest lap. He also took the RAC FF1600 title in his first year of car racing.

Whatever the reason, Ayrton moved into FF2000 with Rushen Green Racing in 1982. He won on each of his Thruxton outings, having played the back markers better than Calvin Fish in August. He clinched both FF2000 titles before his second Thruxton appearance of the year, when he drove a West Surrey Racing F3 Ralt Toyota in November during the City Business Machines TV meeting. Presented with what had been Enrique Mansilla's car, and having performed some discrete adjustments, he put it on pole for his F3 debut, and won by no less than 13 seconds. This televised race prompted a phone call from McLaren's Ron Dennis and, like Tommy the year before, Senna was soon off to Woking for an interview.

In 1983, it was said that the only F3 rival Ayrton took seriously was Martin Brundle, in a similar – but Eddie Jordan run – Ralt-Toyota. In a memorable season of 21 races Senna took pole position 16 times. Ayrton won the first nine races, but Martin steadfastly refused to give up. F3 came to Thruxton no less than five times

*Ayrton Senna showed his pedigree by easily adjusting to his F3 Ralt at Thruxton during several 1983 visits.*

The F3 duel of 1983 has just started. In March Martin Brundle (left) and Ayrton Senna commenced their season-long rivalry.

Ayrton knew Thruxton well from Formula Ford. This is his FF2000 Rushen Green steed in the pit lane in 1982. Was he actually avoiding Tommy Byrne?

that season, and on the first occasion Ayrton proved to be better in the corners and, in winning from pole, successfully conserved his tyres. He beat Brundle by a mere 0.83s. On the second visit, Ayrton beat off American Davy Jones, with Martin unable to comprehend why the Brazilian just didn't make mistakes. Illustrating the Brazilian's dominance, at Thruxton on Easter Monday, Davy Jones became the first driver so far that

season other than Ayrton to lead a complete lap of an F3 race! Visit three provided Ayrton with a victory margin of just four seconds over Martin, but, in September, Ayrton retired with engine failure, blamed on the quality of the fuel; Martin won.

The final race in the 1983 F3 Championship at Thruxton was scheduled for late October, and Martin's dogged determination was reflected in the fact that he

arrived with a single-point lead after 19 rounds. After calculating dropped points, it became clear that Brundle needed to win.

So seriously did Ayrton take this race that he drove his engine down to Novamotor's Italian factory – returning with a powerplant boasting an improved specification. Ron Tauranac had also produced some tweeks for his Ralt cars, but there was only one set of each to go round. Martin received a new pushrod front suspension, whilst Ayrton gained new side pods offering much improved downforce – a distinct advantage around super-fast Thruxton. This divvying up of components led to Martin nicknaming Ayrton 'Sennapod!'

Ayrton's frame of mind was such that he needed a pep talk from Dennis Rushen before annexing pole once the morning mist had cleared. Ingeniously, he taped up his oil radiator outlet to enable his precious engine to warm up quicker. In the race he actually loosened his seat belt so as to be able to remove the tape, whilst Martin found himself boxed in behind Davy Jones. As a result, Ayrton was able to win in front of his proud father on a cloudless day.

Marlboro extended the prize of the F1 test drive to Martin as well as Ayrton, in recognition of his competitiveness. During the year, Senna had attracted sufficient attention to warrant F1 tests with not only Williams, but also McLaren and Brabham, but, in 1984, he actually went off to Toleman to pursue the next part of his eminent career.

*Sitting on the October grid Ayrton had a trick up his sleeve, in addition to new sidepods. Martin Brundle's lead was only a single point.*

## 1984

For 1984, the F3 season was reduced from 20 to 17 races, and a Class B was introduced for one-year-old cars in what was the last season of ground-effect.

The name of Johnny (The Earl of Bute) Dumfries had already appeared on the F3 radar at Thruxton, when he'd come fifth in the opening 1983 race. A year later, Frank Williams' former van driver took a clean sweep of four Thruxton wins.

The initial surprise was when Paul Radisich (Murray Taylor Ralt-VW) took pole for the March race, never having visited the circuit before. Dumfries (Team BP, Dave Price Ralt-VW) had taken the lead, and then won a race made memorable by Mario Hytten's heavy crash at Club. Hytten would later be on the podium for three of Thruxton's 1984 races. In April, Dumfries used special 'delta' front wings on his Ralt. By the end of the season, Ross Cheever became Dumfries' main competitor,

In 1984 Johnny Dumfries utterly dominated at Thruxton with four wins. Unsurprisingly, a Lotus F1 test was already scheduled.

coming home second in the fourth Championship race at Thruxton.

On his way to becoming 1984 British F3 Champion, 24-year-old Dumfries had made a name for himself as a consistent driver who rarely made mistakes. By August, this had already led to a successful 102-lap JPS Lotus-Renault F1 test at Donington.

*One of Johnny's 1984 victories was in March. Here, he's flanked by fellow F3 frontrunners Andrew Gilbert-Scott (left) and Canadian Allen Berg.*

*Ian Taylor had tutored Yorkshireman, Russell Spence who went on to take two Thruxton wins in 1985 in his Warmastyle Reynard (853-VW).*

## 1985

F3 came to Thruxton four times in twelve weeks, with the new flat-bottomed cars generating antagonism as Reynard threatened the Ralt domination and won three times. Yorkshireman Russell Spence won the first two in his Warmastyle Reynard (853-VW), having received intensive training from circuit supremo Ian Taylor. The Ralt teams were unhappy, and unsuccessfully protested the car's nosebox after the first race. In April, having spun off in qualifying, Spence again won in damp conditions, after Andy Wallace stalled at the start. Ralt was enthused

with its first win of the season thanks to Gary Evans in early May in warm conditions. He had taken the lead on the first lap when the similar car of Mauricio Gugelmin had its starter jam on pole. At the end of May, Andy Wallace gave Swallow Racing a one-two, with Tim Davies in second having had a tussle with Spence who ended up in the Allard barriers. In the year when Gugelmin became Champion, Welshman Davies had been on Thruxton's podium each time. Good sized grids characterised the season in which Mancunian Jamaican Carlton Tingling went particularly well at Thruxton in Class B.

In horrendous conditions in 1986, Brazilian Maurizio Sandro Sala 'powerboated' Murray Taylor's Ralt-VW to a well-deserved win.

### 1986

For 1986 there was only one way to go for Andy Wallace – the 1985 F3 Championship runner-up badly needed to win. He did, but not at Thruxton – his Reynard taking the title from Ralt for the first time since 1979, in a season marred by accusations of fuel irregularities throughout the field. Marlboro had departed, and the first two unsponsored Thruxton races were won by Brazilian Maurizio Sandro Sala (Murray Taylor Ralt RT30/86-VW). Silverstone had been snowed off, so Thruxton became the opening race, and no less than

32 drivers took part. It was disappointing that the heavens opened on a day that was not only remembered for some superb BARC marshalling, but also for the F3 debut of Damon Hill. Wallace took the first of two second places which would soon yield a Benetton-BMW F1 test. In the second Thruxton race, Keith Fine brought his Cellnet Ralt RT30/86-Toyota home behind Sala, having repaired it on the grid after going off at Village on one of the warm-up laps. Plucky Dutchman Gerritt van Kouwen won the third Thruxton F3 round of the year.

## 1987

In 1987 Eddie Jordan Racing finally won the British F3 Championship, with star driver Johnny Herbert, team manager Dave Benbow, a Reynard 873 chassis, and the engine of the year – the Spiess VW – which was said to have 20bhp more than the opposition. For the second year running inclement Silverstone weather meant that Thruxton started the season – it would close it, too. The new track surface was found to be slippery, but *Autocourse* correctly described Herbert as 'pulverising' the opposition whilst mastering it. He still had wheelspin from his pole position start, and, having dropped back, eventually took a seven-second lead from Bertrand Gachot, who was with F3 returnee WSR. Herbert also beat Dave Scott's 1981 lap record, with 1m11.45s – 118.70mph/191.03kmh. He won the second Thruxton race, too, from the Alfa Romeo-powered Reynard of Thomas Danielsson. Both drivers had fought hard with Gachot, and Danielsson was even put on the grass at 140mph approaching the chicane. For the third Thruxton race, Gachot had swapped his VW engine in his Ralt RT31 for an Alfa, only to collide with Herbert at Church. Herbert had already missed a gear passing the pits on lap two, and this time Danielsson was able to take his first British F3 win. Perhaps Herbert's greatest drive was at the closing race when, having collided with Danielsson at the Complex on the first lap, he dropped to last. After a magnificent recovery, he finished third, lowering the lap record once again (1m11.16s – 119.19mph/191.82kph). Gachot took his third win of the season.

*On the ladder to F1, twenty three year-old Johnny Herbert at last gave Eddie Jordan an F3 Championship in 1987 – and two Thruxton wins.*

The first lap of the first F3 race of 1987 at Campbell, Romford's Johnny Herbert leads on the new Tarmac surface

In front of Finnish flags at Club, JJ Lehto started his winning ways in March, giving the Tom's Toyota engine its first win at Thruxton. It was actually a one-two-three for Tom's. Martin Donnelly, in the Intersport (Cellnet-Ricoh) Ralt RT32, took pole and fastest lap, but in changing from second to fifth gear at Campbell lost the advantage, and had to settle for second place. Paul Warwick was making a name for himself in his EJR machine.

At a sunny round three of the Championship at Easter, Paul Warwick was third, Donnelly won, and Gary Brabham second. In trying to pass Donnelly on lap three, Lehto struck the Club barriers a hefty blow, injuring a rib, and joined his Pacific team-mate Evian Demoulas – who had shunted in qualifying – for a brief stay in Salisbury hospital. Damon Hill, meanwhile, had taken a new F3 lap record (1m11.07s – 119.34mph/192.06kph) before having a 135mph grassy scare at Church which cost him the lead.

Damon took his first win of the year in May from pole in what was a very wet race. This time Lehto went off into the Allard barriers, and Donnelly, who was trying a special differential more suited to dry conditions, came third behind Gary Brabham. In September, Brabhams ruled! Gary won the main race (Bowman/NEC Ralt RT32), with David Brabham taking the Class B spoils. Macau-winner Gary got off the line best and, controversially, banged wheels with Lehto who came second in front of Hill.

## 1988

A different driver won each of the four F3 visits to Thruxton in 1988, a year in which Ralt and Reynard continued their rivalry, and Keith Wiggins' Pacific Racing came in from Formula Ford with Finn Jyri Jarvilehto taking the overall Championship through sheer consistency.

The busy F3 pit lane in 1988, with Gary Brabham's NEC Team Brabham Ralt RT32/Spiess waiting patiently in the foreground.

### 1989

In the last year of the decade competition was so rife in F3 that protests over the legitimacy of VW-Spiess and Mugen Honda engines soured the atmosphere. John Alcorn was a lucky man, surviving a huge somersault at Kimpton in testing, after making contact with Warwick Rooklyn.

A year earlier there had been some concern that the Vauxhall Lotus Challenge would take competitors away from F3, but this proved not to be the case, and, in 1989, the first graduates from that series moved into the Lucas British F3 Championship. Chief amongst these was Alan McNish (Ralt RT33 Mugen Honda), who won two of Thruxton's three F3 races. This was only after Swede Rickard Rydell had dominated the first round, when both McNish and his team-mate Mika Hakkinen stalled at the start. Gary Ayles came third, after a clash with Steve Robertson on Woodham Hill. At round six (Thruxton race two) Dick Bennetts scored a one-two in both qualifying and in the race – Alan McNish won and Derek Higgins came second with the fastest lap. David Brabham had to be helped out of his car after qualifying, thanks to food poisoning, but still managed third place. The race had to be stopped early-on when eight cars went off at the Complex. After the restart, Damon Hill belted the polystyrene blocks at the chicane, following brake problems, and retired. David Brabham came to October's round 15 (Thruxton race three) with a chance of the title, but collided with Derek Higgins and smote the barriers at the Complex, ending such hopes. Alan McNish won the race and the title, with Rydell and Robertson following him home on the road.

*Jackie Stewart in 1989 at Thruxton, supporting his son Paul's (right) F3 campaign. Jackie knew the track very well from his F2 days.*

Dumfries' Allan McNish had progressed from being 1988 Vauxhall Lotus Champion to take two Thruxton F3 wins in 1989.
Formula 1 and Le Mans beckoned.

Damon Hill having a rare F3 off at Club in 1989, having hit the polystyrene blocks thanks to brake failure.

So, F3's decade closed with the Formula in rude health. At the May meeting there had been no less than 36 drivers taking part, and the prospect for the '90s looked rosy. F3 had produced numerous F1 drivers and, in cutting their teeth at Thruxton in the '80s, some had added sufficient expertise to help them become World Champions in the '90s.

Damon Hill's car racing debut. The future World Champion started from the very back of the FF2000 grid in November 1983.

# British Touring Cars

Boasting road car look-alikes, the British Saloon Car Championship, today referred to as the British Touring Car Championship (BTCC), was a firm crowd-pleaser throughout the '80s. Whilst politics and the economy would influence the series, one Thruxton driver would remain a constant throughout the decade – Andy Rouse.

For 1980, the Tricentrol backed Group 1 series boasted a new top class capacity limit of 3500cc, to encourage competitors to take on the '70s dominatrix – the 3-litre Ford Capri. Eventually, the Rover SDI V8 would be sufficiently honed to win at Thruxton, but not in 1980, when Gordon Spice's GSR Capri won both races. In April, 28 cars were entered, and the pole-sitting Spice led home early leader Bristolian Vince Woodman (Esso Capri) after previous leader Andy Rouse (second GSR Capri) had collided with Derrick Brunt's Vauxhall. Eventual Champion, Weymouth's Win Percy, was third in his Pentax Mazda RX7. Elsewhere, Stirling Moss had his second race in an Audi 1.6 80GLE – 18 years after his near-fatal accident at Goodwood – and Martin Brundle fielded a Toyota Celica. Local drivers – Salisbury's Alan Curnow and Christchurch's Richard Longman – lowered the Class D lap record during the season with their Fiestas. Five months after the first race, Woodman took pole and briefly led before suffering engine failure, as GSR took its fifth successive one-two of the season. As a portent of things to come, in 1981 Jeff Allam's 3.5 Rover V8 came third.

*Coventry-based preparation expert Andy Rouse was constantly at the head of Thruxton's BTCC field throughout the 1980s.*

A classic confrontation with Andy Rouse's scarlet GSR Capri dicing with Vince Woodman's white Esso version in 1980.

Win Percy's TWR Mazda RX7 – seen here in 1981 – was a controversial BTCC entry but it still took him to two titles.

Allam's *Daily Express* Rover won Thruxton's second 1981 BTCC race to break the two-year Ford Capri stranglehold. The May Tricentrol visit had been characterised by new lap records in all classes, and a Capri one-two-three. Jonathan Buncombe had been going well but, following a puncture on lap 11, re-joined the race just behind team-mate Woodman only to be accused of shielding the race winner. Behind were the GSR Capris of Spice, who had made a bad start, and Rouse. Racing without team orders, there was more than a little contact between the two. In September Jeff Allam drove without challenge from the outside of the front row to the flag, ahead of Win Percy's Mazda and Peter Lovett's Rover. Tom Walkinshaw Racing (TWR) cleaned up with these first three cars, whilst

its other drivers, Martin Brundle, Stirling Moss, and Chuck Nicholson, all fared well in their respective classes. Percy became BTCC Champion-elect for the second year running, and unexpectedly announced his retirement in the paddock.

Percy 'unretired' for 1982, only to win the Championship in his 1.6 Toyota Corolla. Thruxton provided a Vince Woodman double, with GSR's Gordon Spice and Andy Rouse standing on the podium both times, too, in what would be the team's final BTCC season. In April, Jeff Allam's Rover had been on pole, only for his tyres to shred in the race before finishing fourth. Steve Soper won the up-to-1300cc class in his Metro. In May, Woodman and former F2 Thruxton winner Rad Dougall (Rover) had a momentous fight.

From Tolpuddle in Dorset – of the Tolpuddle Martyrs fame – Win Percy repeated history by visiting Australia to race at Bathurst. Thruxton was his home circuit.

Barrie 'Whizzo' Williams brightened up the BTCC in 1981 when he raced a Colt for old school friend Ted Hughes.

For 1983 Group 1 was replaced by the three-class Group A, and Tricentrol had become Trimoco. Wiltshire Porsche dealer Peter Lovett won both Thruxton races on the road in his TWR Rover Vitesse, but all was not well in a season marred by eligibility protests. At the second round both Lovett and Jeff Allam's similar TWR Rover were excluded – a decision that was appealed and which amazingly wouldn't be concluded until midway through

*Usually remembered for driving Fords and Rovers, Andy Rouse also raced a BTCC Alfa Romeo GTV6 in 1983.*

*Wiltshire's Peter Lovett appeared to clean up at Thruxton in 1983 when he 'won' both races on the road for Rover.*

*Steve Soper may have won the May 1984 race on the road, but technical eligibility allegations surrounded the result.*

the following season. The scrutineering bay at the end of that second race was filled with protested cars – one of the all time lows of the BTCC.

By 1984 Rovers were firmly stamping their authority on a circuit that plainly suited them. Andy Rouse took a lap record and a pole-to-flag victory in his self-engineered ICS Vitesse in April ahead of Tony Pond and Peter Lovett in similar TWR machines. In May Steve Soper (Rover) came first, this time ahead of three other Rovers in the hands of Rouse, Pond and Jean-Louis Schlesser. The race is not only remembered for extensive body damage

*Steve Soper is seen here in happier times blasting off the STP Modified Sports front row in 1980 in his famous Radbourne Fiat X19.*

*'Soperman' was back in 1988 to take his Eggenberger Sierra to a resounding victory.*

throughout the field but also for the absence of the winner on the podium – he had been taken straight to scrutineering for his car to be re-examined. Rouse was the 1984 Champion but Rover's unhappiness saw it completely withdraw from the series mid-season, whilst also relinquishing its claim to the 1983 title.

At Thruxton in 1985 you needed a turbo to win. Dave Brodie possessed just such a powerplant in his Colt Starion which took him to pole in April – by a margin of 3s. Andy Rouse's turbo-powered Sierra triumphed in the second race. In both events Neil McGrath's Rover came second having fought hard with Frank Sytner's BMW first time out, in a race which featured a spectacular crash opposite the pits, involving Rob Kirby's Alfa and Graham Goode's Nissan. Talk of the year was the appearance of motorcycling ace Barry Sheene who promisingly finished third in April in his 2.8 Toyota Celica Supra, only to be part of a race-stopping Allard accident in May. He was lucky to emerge from his banana-shaped car with only a damaged foot, having been T-boned in the five car shunt. Only ten cars could re-start. Rouse would again be Champion, winning nine of the year's eleven events.

Chris Hodgetts would be BTCC Champion in both 1986 and 1987, ending Andy Rouse's three-year reign. In the sole 1986 Thruxton race Mike Newman broke the mould by taking a very popular win in his BMW 635

after early leader Rouse had spun luridly at Church – Rouse would come second ahead of Rob Kirby's Alfa – and Dennis Leech had engine failure after taking the lap record. Richard Longman's Datapost Escort RS Turbo had been up at the front too, before fuel starvation hit his chances.

Dennis Leech's black and orange Rover Vitesse was finally victorious in 1987 for the first Dunlop-sponsored Thruxton Championship race, ahead of the Sierra of Graham Goode and David Carvell's Rover. West Countryman Leech was driving with an injured hand following a lawn mower accident, and only Graham Scarborough's Rover posed a threat before he retired. Champion-elect, Chris Hodgetts, had a big off at Church

In 1987 the injured West Countryman Dennis Leech was a popular winner in his Rover.

71

Former F1 driver Guy Edwards is nudged into a spin at Club in 1989.

in practice on a day when only 15 cars raced. Radio 210 Raceday in May was sunny, and Andy Rouse was back on top of the Thruxton podium having wisely selected hard tyres, which helped him fight off Tim Harvey's second-placed Istel Rover. David Carvell's Rover was again third.

Steve 'Soperman' Soper returned for 1988 on May 2, and he, too, used hard Pirellis on his new Eggenberger Sierra Cosworth. Noticeably superior in Thruxton's long corners he fought off Rouse's record-breaking Sierra after the latter had to pit with a puncture – both commentated for the BBC from their cockpits. It was exactly four years since the two drivers had a similar confrontation at Thruxton.

Now the Esso RAC Championship, the BTCC's final two races of the decade in 1989, were bittersweet for Dave Brodie who won the first race on the road in his BBR Sierra, and led the second only to be disqualified following fuel problems. Tim Harvey was, therefore, victorious at the start of May in his Sierra RS500 ahead of the similar cars of Karl Jones and Mike Newman. Andy Rouse had led until his engine cut out. Rolling starts were an innovation, even if some of the drivers were not terribly disciplined. Qualifying was made interesting after 1988 Champion Frank Sytner had upended his 2.3 BMW M3 at Allard. This left just over three minutes of frantic action for the drivers to set their best times.

*Andy Rouse finished the decade on Thruxton's front row in his Kaliber Sierra. On this 1989 May Day he would notch up another win.*

At the end of May Andy Rouse was appropriately triumphant on a hot and sunny day. He was harried by Tim Harvey's Sierra but the race was stopped just as the latter was homing in. Rob Gravett had completely totalled his Sierra at Segrave following a clash with Phil Dowsett's Corolla. In a year when John Cleland would be the final Champion of the decade, in his Vauxhall Astra, promisingly large fields became commonplace but the series was again characterised by eligibility arguments off the track.

# Significant others

Thousands of racing miles occurred during the decade, with the highlights including the final two 1980 races of the Aurora AFX British F1 Championship. Whilst Eliseo Salazar won both in his Williams FW07, Ray Mallock had a high speed fiery accident which destroyed his Surtees TS20 at Goodwood in May. He later generously rewarded those BARC marshals who had rescued him.

Following the demise of Aurora AFX, F1 appearances were mainly restricted to the popular Brooklands Racedays, in events such as those for Pre '70 and '71 single-seaters. John Foulston was often dominant in his McLaren M19A and Can Am McLarens in those evocative sports car races, sometimes sponsored by his own Atlantic Computers business or by Willhire. The main picture on the front cover of this book shows him chasing Ray Mallock's glorious pole-sitting Lola T70. In May 1984 Foulston actually won three races at a single meeting. Another notable F1 appearance was that of John Watson, who demonstrated a McLaren-Honda MP4 at the celebratory meeting for McLaren-Honda's 1988 F1 constructor's victory.

Shrill F1 Williams dominated the October 1980 Aurora AFX start. Eliseo Salazar (FW07) leads away Emilio de Villota (FW07) and Giacomo Agostini (FW06).

In 1985 at the Brooklands Raceday pre-1970 single-seaters included both thunderous F1 and F5000 cars. John Foulston won in his F1 McLaren M19A.

John Watson demonstrated an F1 McLaren MP4/3 in 1988.
He recorded a 1m 09s lap. (See also the front cover.)

David Auger's beautiful Gulf Mirage BRM Mk 2 (12) jumps
John Foulston's McLaren M1B (4) in the 1981 Willhire Historic
GT race at May's Brooklands Raceday.

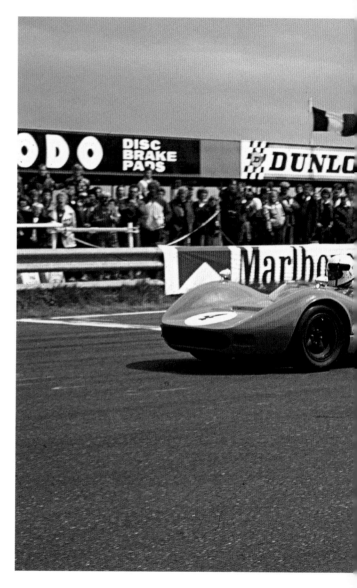

John Foulston was famed for the way he tamed his McLaren M8C Can Am, here winning the 1985 Failsafe Historic GT race.

A Thundersports hot seat! Chester Wedgwood's sponsor would have been pleased with such an association in 1985. Chester probably wasn't!

The first Formula Vauxhall Lotus start in 1988. The red and white cars of housemates and future F1 drivers Allan McNish and Mika Hakkinen triumphed.

Advised by fellow Finn Keke Rosberg, a youthful Mika Hakkinen won the 1988 Opel-Lotus Euroseries, and was runner-up in the UK equivalent for Dragon Motorsport.

During the decade, four new series actually started at the circuit. Formula First and Formula Renault – later a stalwart of the BARC – kicked off in 1988 and 1989 respectively. The inaugural General Motors Vauxhall Lotus Challenge was launched at Thruxton in 1988. There were unfounded fears that the reward of an F3000 test drive for the winner and a £60,000 prize might adversely affect F3's healthy grids.

The inaugural Renault 5 Turbo race was won by Jonathan Palmer. Such a cavalry charge concentrated the minds of the BARC's marshals at Allard!

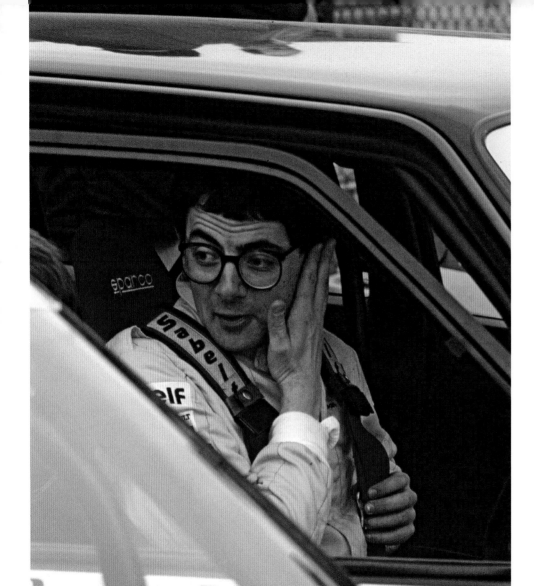

The first ever Renault 5 Turbo race was won by Jonathan Palmer in 1985 in a series which later included none other than celebrated TV celebrity Rowan Atkinson who had been tutored by Gerry Marshall. The Renaults produced great action and, in common with other one-make Championships, sometimes proved top heavy at Club!

Mr Bean or Blackadder? TV celebrity Rowan Atkinson was a frequent understated competitor in Renault 5s, and is seen here in 1988.

Club corner's high kerbs frequently catch the unwary. Here, Lionel Wiffen's Renault 5 capsizes in 1989 ...

... whilst a Mini Metro went flying in 1984. It didn't roll!

*Early product placement? Great crowd favourite Gerry Marshall samples his perfect reward having notched up another Monroe win in 1980 in his Production Saloon Capri.*

Club racing legend Gerry Marshall was well into the production saloon phase of his career, fielding his 3-litre Capri and taking no fewer than 11 wins on a circuit that was a personal favourite. He would later race an Opel Monza, a Saab Turbo, and even a Shell Super Talbot Sunbeam in a celebrity event at Thruxton.

Gerry is most remembered for his large Super Saloon Vauxhalls of the '70s, and the leading exponent of these exciting vehicles at the start of the '80s was Boston's Tony Dickinson – a multiple Thruxton winner in the Wendy Wools Championships. Another circuit favourite was Newbury's Ian Taylor, who presided over the circuit's Racing School, and who would always be up front in Sports 200 before moving on to Formula Atlantic.

*Thruxton was a personal driving favourite of Gerry Marshall, and in 1981 he took three production saloon wins in this Autoplan 3-litre Ford Capri.*

## Significant others

Boston's Tony Dickinson was a prodigious special saloon winner at Thruxton and, with his unique Skoda, was a national hero in Czechoslovakia.

Boasting a Lola Sports 2000 chassis, Tony Dickinson's Skoda S110R special saloon – seen here in 1980 – was powered by an F2 Hart 4230R engine.

Few knew Thruxton better than Racing School supremo Ian Taylor. From a distinguished single-seater background, here he celebrates a 1980 Sports 2000 victory.

Ian Taylor's Sports 2000 Queensgate Tiga SC80 took 12 wins during 1980, as well as Thruxton's lap record for the class.

# Formula Ford and The Race of the Decade

Throughout the decade hordes of equally-matched Formula Ford 1600cc single-seaters guaranteed maximum excitement for the Thruxton crowds. Being relatively cheap, the class was a recognised starting place for the new young talent from karting headed toward the top of the sport.

Notable Formula Ford race winners included Rick Morris, Tommy Byrne, Jim Walsh, Andrew Gilbert-Scott, Enrique Mansilla, Mauricio Gugelmin, Julian Bailey, Peter Hardman, Dave Coyne, John Pratt, John Booth, Jason Elliott, Paul Warwick, Phil Andrews, Derek Higgins, Alain Menu, Kurt Luby, and Kelvin Burt

Future F1 household names included Ayrton da Silva, Jonathan Palmer, Bertrand Gachot, Damon Hill, Eddie Irvine, and David Coulthard, who actually won his first car race at Thruxton in 1987 – that season he won no fewer than 22 times from 28 starts.

Thanks to loyal sponsor Ricoh, Damon Hill was a frontrunner in the major FF1600 Championships in 1985.

Eddie Irvine's works Duckhams Van Diemen took both the RAC and Esso FF1600 Championships in 1987, with 19 wins from 36 starts.

David Coulthard won his first ever Formula Ford race at Thruxton in 1989, and was the inaugural McLaren Autosport BRDC Young Driver Award winner.

'Race of the Decade' winner John Pratt said his Team BP Reynard Minister 84FF was both "... easy to drive and put the power down well."

### The Race of the Decade –
### Townsend Thoresen Formula Ford 1600 race, July 8th 1984

Arguably the race of most historic significance was that already well-chronicled F3 showdown between Ayrton Senna and Martin Brundle in 1983, but, for sheer excitement, one particular Formula Ford race still sticks firmly in the mind. At the time even *Autosport's* Marcus Pye described it as: "... the finest encounter of the decade," and to this observer it was never topped.

The memorable contest was between the evenly matched Duckhams Van Diemen of Dave Coyne and the BP-backed Reynard of John Pratt, during which the lead would constantly change. It was anyone's guess as to who would win until the final corner.

Dave Coyne recalls: "I came second by 0.19s. John let me through on the final tour and then slipstreamed back past me. Quite honestly I made a mistake going into the Complex by going past John."

John Pratt's version was: "Although there were five cars involved at the front it was mainly between Dave and myself. All the other cars were just behind us but were swapping places all the time. For the first quarter of the race it was Mark Peters and then Dave caught up

Three abreast at Club. Dave Coyne pushes down the inside of John Pratt in the middle, and Mark Peters forces around the outside.

and it was the two of us for the rest of the race. It was simply the case that twice a lap we would change places whilst each of us was desperately looking for the break which never came. On the last lap I was leading into the Complex and I allowed him to go past me so that I could take the tow from him coming out of Church. Even though I overtook coming up the straight I was still very worried about Dave on the brakes as I was expecting him to come around outside of me, but luckily he didn't!"

# Also from Veloce –

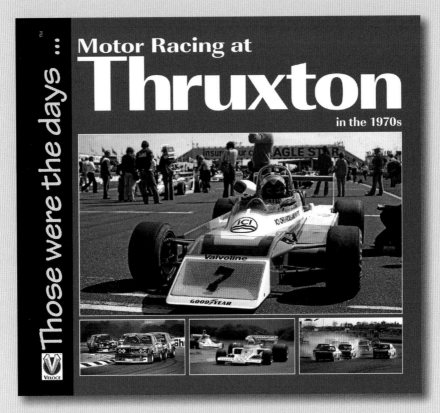

ISBN: 978-1-845843-70-0
Paperback • 19x20.5cm • £14.99* UK/$29.99* USA • 96 pages • 100 colour and b&w pictures

Featuring many previously unpublished photographs from the author's personal collection, this is an insightful account of '70s racing at one of the fastest motor racing circuits in the UK.

For more info on Veloce titles, visit our website at www.veloce.co.uk • email: info@veloce.co.uk • Tel: +44(0)1305 260068
* prices subject to change, p&p extra

# Also from Veloce –

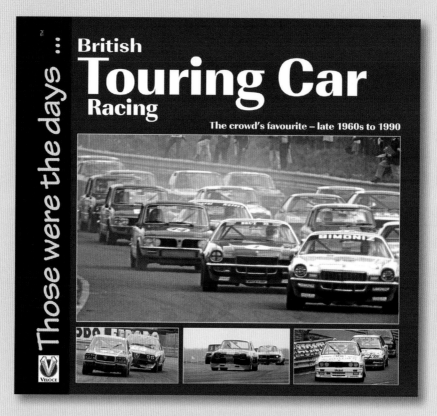

ISBN: 978-1-845842-47-5

Paperback • 19x20.5cm • £14.99* UK/$29.95* USA • 96 pages • 36 colour and b&w pictures

Evocative pictures of British Touring Car racing – the crowd's favourite – from the flares of the late 1960s to the turbos of 1990. Features shots of all aspects of the racing – the drivers, the cars, the paddocks, and more.

For more info on Veloce titles, visit our website at www.veloce.co.uk • email: info@veloce.co.uk • Tel: +44(0)1305 260068
* prices subject to change, p&p extra

# Also from Veloce –

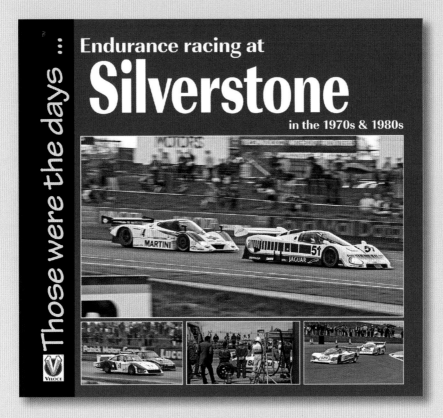

ISBN: 978-1-845842-77-2

Paperback • 19x20.5cm • £14.99* UK/$29.95* USA • 96 pages • 125 colour and b&w pictures

This book charts the progress of the Silverstone 6-hour and 1000km races, year-by-year from 1976, through the era of the Group C cars, up to the end of the eighties, with previously unpublished accounts and photographs of each event.

For more info on Veloce titles, visit our website at www.veloce.co.uk • email: info@veloce.co.uk • Tel: +44(0)1305 260068
* prices subject to change, p&p extra

# Index